MW00622844

NO-FAIL HABITS

NO-FAIL HABITS

Design the Daily Rituals that Help You Win at Work and Succeed at Life

By the editors of

MICHAEL HYATT & CO.

Franklin, Tennessee

No-Fail Habits
Copyright © 2020 by Michael Hyatt & Co.
Published by Michael Hyatt & Co.

All rights reserved. No part of this publication may be reproduced, stored in a retrieval system, or transmitted in any form or by any means without written permission of the publisher.

Bulk orders for your team? Email sales@michaelhyatt.com.

ISBN: 978-1-7353817-0-1
Printed in the United States of America

MichaelHyatt.com

CONTENTS

Introduction 7

Chapter 1: Autopilot for Your Brain 9

Self-Automation Level 1:
Create Habits to Automate Single Tasks

Chapter 2: Leveraging the Power of Your Subconscious 21

Chapter 3: How to Form a Habit 35

Self-Automation Level 2:
Leverage Rituals to Automate Multiple Tasks

Chapter 4: How Rituals Set You Up for Success 53

Chapter 5: Taking Daily Rituals to the Next Level 67

Chapter 6: Using Rituals to Manage Your Energy 79

Self-Automation Level 3:
Design Templates to Automate Entire Days

Chapter 7: Design the Day 97

Chapter 8: Batch the Tasks 111

Chapter 9: Install the Template 123

Sources 137

About Michael Hyatt & Co. 141

Introduction

As a high achiever, you know exactly what you want to accomplish. But the week hits hard. By noon on Monday, you're in reaction mode, responding to problems, urgent messages, and interruptions. By Wednesday, you're playing for time, hoping the weekend will give you a reboot. It's demoralizing. Why is it so hard to get through a single day without getting thrown off track?

It doesn't have to be. With over a century of combined experience in business leadership, the team at Michael Hyatt & Co. has cracked the productivity code. Together, we've built one of the fastest-growing companies in the country without sacrificing our families, well-being, or creative pursuits. We've learned that the key to productivity isn't a "work hard, play never" grind. Instead, it is implementing a system of strong habits that structure your day, allowing you to automate your most important activities and make you more productive in less time.

In *No-Fail Habits,* we'll teach you the science behind self-automation. You'll learn how to hack your brain, take back your time, and feel equipped to handle whatever gets thrown at you from Monday to Sunday.

With *No-Fail Habits,* you'll go from ending each day wondering "What just happened?" to executing on your intentions, reaching your goals, and achieving more than you ever thought possible. Let's start by addressing why communication is difficult, and what we can do about it. Everyone faces three basic challenges in communication. I'll bet you recognize yourself or someone you know in each of them.

1

Autopilot for Your Brain

By making some decisions a matter of routine, you free yourself to focus on your highest priorities without neglecting other responsibilities.

Chief Operating Officer is a busy and sometimes stressful job in any company. That's especially true when a company is growing rapidly and introducing lots of new products. Megan Hyatt Miller, COO of Michael Hyatt & Co., experienced all the highs of being COO. During her tenure, the company has been named to the Inc. 5000 list of fastest-growing privately held companies for three years in a row, consistently had revenue increases above 50 percent annually, and grown from a handful of contractors and part-timers to a team of thirty-five (and growing) full-time employees. It used to be especially hectic for Megan, who is also a mom to five children. "I vividly remember the moment all the complexities caught up with me," Megan recalls. "It happened when I saw this sidewalk sign announcing 'Muffins with Mom.'"

The day began with a flurry of activity that's standard in the Miller household. There were kids to get ready for school, breakfasts to prepare, and a full slate of activity ahead. For Megan and her husband, Joel, all of that is usually no problem—just par for the course. But on this day, Megan was scheduled to travel on company business. Between the flight schedule and Nashville traffic, she barely had time to get dressed, help get the kids ready, and make it out the door.

"Want me to drive Moses to school?" Joel asked.

"No, I can still do it. But only if we leave right now." With that, she and Moses hopped in the car and dashed off to the elementary school. "It was going to be almost a drive-by," Megan remembers. "I knew I'd barely have time to pull through the drop-off line before heading to the airport."

Pulling up, she saw the sandwich board on the school sidewalk announcing that this was the day for Muffins with Mom in Moses's second-grade class. As the car rolled to a stop, Megan noticed a dozen or so moms, all carrying baked goods, heading inside. With a hurried apology to Moses, Megan wished him a good day and drove off to catch her flight.

"I had completely forgotten the event," Megan said. "I was in tears all the way to the airport, thinking how disappointed and embarrassed Moses would be. The only child there without his mom. I just knew I'd given him all the talking points he'd need to explain to some future therapist how I'd ruined his life."

You may have had a similar, if less dramatic, experience—that moment when the intricacies of your calendar finally catch up to you. Maybe you forgot that a meeting was canceled and wasted half an hour driving. Or you overslept and left your workout partner in the lurch. Or you get a pop-up reminder for a meeting that starts in five minutes, which you thought was next week. Ironically, it's the seemingly small details that trigger these bigger breakdowns.

When that happens, it feels like you have to make a choice between being a high achiever and living a balanced life. The more you try to accomplish, the more incompetent you feel. That's probably why you picked up this book. The stress of managing too many appointments, projects, and responsibilities has finally caught up to you. Something's got to give.

For Megan, the Great Muffin Debacle became a turning point. "It's when I realized I'd lost control of my priorities and my schedule," she said. "The things that mattered most to me were slipping away." She decided to do something about it.

You can, too. We want you to win at work *and* succeed in life. You do not have to make a choice between being a high achiever *or* having a full and satisfying life. One of the keys to this Double Win, as we call it, is the practice of self-automation.

The Easiest Way to Fly

Self-automation is the process of putting some of your daily decisions and actions on autopilot, so they happen without conscious thought. This allows you to manage important details of your life while freeing mental bandwidth to focus on other priorities.

As a high achiever, you're a bit like the pilot of your own plane. You're the one in control and each day is like a new flight. When you were younger, all the "flights" were often pretty simple. You probably didn't give much thought to organizing each day.

But life gets complicated the older you get. You may embark on a career, or get married, or start a business. Perhaps you're simultaneously completing your education and working full-time or volunteering your time while also navigating daycare and sports schedules. It's like going from flying a Cessna 150 to the cockpit of a Boeing 777. You now have highly complex responsibilities. People are depending on you. There are more details to manage than ever before. While you're doing essentially the same thing—piloting your own life—it is a lot more challenging. Carrying all the information in your head while managing thousands of decisions each day becomes an overwhelming, if not impossible, task.

Remember, though, that commercial pilots are able to fly incredibly complex planes very long distances every single day. Even with a copilot, that's a huge challenge. How do they manage by themselves?

Actually, they don't.

For over a century, many airplanes have been equipped with autopiloting systems to handle routine tasks such as maintaining course, speed, and altitude. Today's more advanced systems can do everything except taxi and takeoff, including landing the plane. So, what does the pilot do? Plenty.

Veteran pilot Paul Templeton explains it this way. "During cruise flight, the pilots are busy monitoring the route and the destination's weather, keeping track of the fuel burn, coordinating any changes with their dispatcher, talking with air traffic control, and when over the ocean and not in radar contact, making position reports. It would be very difficult to manage all of the above while actively hand-flying the airplane. Autopilot frees us up, enabling us to manage other aspects of the flight."

With the help of autopilot, the captain and co-captain can handle a much more complex airplane over a far longer flight than they ever could on their own. With the autopilot engaged, they are free to focus on what matters most—controlling the overall function of the plane and getting their passengers safely to the destination. They accomplish more with less effort.

Self-automation can do the same for you. This book is about leveraging the power of self-automation to free your brain, manage your focus, and get your most important tasks done. It will lighten the daily burden of managing your life, allowing you to focus energy and attention on your highest priorities.

How does self-automation work? It looks like:

- Creating a workday start-up routine so minor administrative tasks don't bleed into your most productive hours.
- Populating tomorrow's task list before leaving the office to ensure you get a running start in the morning.
- Keeping a standing appointment to run with a friend every morning at 6:00 a.m., eliminating daily decisions on if, when, and where to run.
- Using email filters that route messages from certain senders directly to your assistant, reducing your time spent on communication.
- Having your assistant schedule all internal meetings on Mondays so most days are free to focus on high-leverage tasks.
- Emptying your inboxes before diving into a complex task so you aren't pinged with questions distracting you from the work at hand.
- Preparing a week's worth of meals at once so you don't have to think about what to cook on busy weeknights.
- Scheduling your time off for the coming year in December so you won't have to choose between

personal rejuvenation and known deadlines throughout the year.

Perhaps you're already using some of these simple tactics. They're really just the tip of the self-automation iceberg, though. When you're finished reading this book, you'll know how to leverage the habit loop to self-automate any action you choose. When you understand how to create complex habit chains, called rituals, you can feel successful before your day even begins. And this book is full of templates you can design to sail through each day without breaking focus.

As a result, you'll see an immediate boost in your energy and productivity. And you'll have perfect confidence that your most important priorities are taken care of. In short, this book can help you regain control of your life.

The Flight Plan

There are three levels of self-automation in this book. In Level 1, you'll learn about the basic building block of self-automation, your habits. Understanding how they work is what makes them so powerful. And we'll show you how to form or break any habit you choose.

Level 2 is a deep dive into the second level of habit formation, Daily Rituals. Learn to master the four basic rituals that form the foundation of a productive day. And you'll discover how to use rituals to manage your most precious resource, your mental energy. Finally, Level 2 shares a simple formula for installing any ritual, ensuring that your self-automation efforts get off the ground.

Level 3 takes self-automation beyond single behaviors to entire days. By separating the three contexts in which all of your activity takes place, you'll discover a simple way to match your best energy with the most demanding tasks. This level covers the four types of batching you can set up in your day. Institute batching and each day will run smoothly without the need for constant decision making. Finally, you'll identify four steps to create your ideal day that contains wins both in work and in your personal endeavors.

By learning to make fewer decisions every day, you can actually accomplish much more while doing less. Ready to start the journey? Let's begin by learning the surprising science behind self-automation and what that means for you.

MOMENTUM BUILDER

Clarify the Problem

You will learn a lot from this book just by reading it. But don't let it stop there. Put that knowledge to work transforming your life.

Each chapter closes with a challenge to help you build momentum with self-automation. Complete each Momentum Builder before reading the next chapter. When you're done, you'll have a solid start on automating your life, and how exactly to complete it.

Your first step is to clarify the problem. If you've chosen to read this book, you're likely looking for a solution. To what? Write a paragraph or bulleted list about the pain points that you'd like to address. What feels out of control? Why do you want to learn about habits and rituals? What does it feel like to be you right now?

Write freely. This is for your eyes only.

SELF-AUTOMATION

LEVEL 1

Create Habits to Automate Single Tasks

2

Leveraging the Power of Your Subconscious

Self-automation works by transferring routine decisions and tasks to your subconscious, freeing you to focus on higher priorities.

Our founder and CEO, Michael Hyatt, discovered the power of habits when he decided to run a half marathon many years ago. He started by signing up for Nashville's Music City Marathon. Then, in a flash of inspiration, he made his decision public and invited all his employees at Thomas Nelson Publishing to join him. "At that point, there was no going back," Michael said. "I created a training plan, picked up some running shoes, and got to work. I can't tell you how many times I was greeted by his assistant with a pained expression. 'I'm so sorry,' she'd say. 'He had to step out.' Or, 'He just let me know he can't meet today.' Or, 'He's in another meeting.' Not only did he cancel most of our meetings, but he did so without notice—and then had his assistant break the news."

Week one of training was a success. Still riding the high from signing up and inspiring his team, he exceeded his running goals. Week two was tougher, but a few morning pep-talks later, and he'd managed to complete his mileage. When business travel undermined his routine during week three, Michael recommitted to getting back on track. Then came week four.

That Monday morning found Michael exhausted from being on the road and still sore from the past few weeks of training. The struggle to get out of bed was over before it started. He rolled over and went back to sleep, telling himself there was plenty of time to catch up later. Tuesday morning brought a couple of urgent emails that demanded attention before breakfast. Wednesday snuck by without a run. Before he knew it, Michael was running only once or twice a week. Just weeks away from a 13.1-mile race, his performance was declining, not improving.

Michael recalls being totally discouraged. "The worst part was I couldn't figure out why I couldn't power my way through this."

Willpower Doesn't Work

There's a simple reason for Michael's decline even though he started out strong. He was relying mostly on willpower to get him out of bed and into his running shoes. And willpower doesn't work. At least, not for long. It simply takes too much, well, willpower to override your body's basic disposition day after day. The part of your brain that controls your conscious choices simply doesn't have that much horsepower. And science proves it.

When you consciously make decisions and act on them, which is essentially what willpower is, you're drawing on what neuroscientists call *executive function.* This function is governed by the prefrontal cortex of your brain. Making choices is literally top of mind, as the saying goes. But most of your body's functions, even elective actions, have nothing to do with executive function. They are governed by a vast network of subconscious controls. And these systems are highly resistant to executive control. In other words, willpower can't touch them, or at least not for long.

Try holding your breath. The world record is an amazing 22 minutes, 22 seconds, but the average person can last only about 2 minutes. At a certain point, your medulla oblongata, the part of your brain that controls breathing, blood pressure, heart rhythms, among other things, will say, "That's enough!" You'll start breathing again whether you want to or not.

Willpower is good for short bursts of intense focus. But it demands too much of your brain's processing power to be effective for long. To ensure that you take a certain action consistently, you need something more powerful. You need to tap the part of your brain that does things automatically, without having to make a decision about the action constantly. When you do, you'll find yourself relying on willpower less, not more. You'll also accomplish more than ever before. The results are simply amazing.

The Power of Habits

After realizing he didn't have the willpower to train for the half-marathon, Michael hit on another strategy. Every night before going to bed, he got his running gear out of the closet and laid it in a tidy stack directly in front of the bathroom door. Now, changing into running gear required no decision—quite the opposite. If Michael decided not to run, he would have to step over his running shoes and make the choice to put them away. Avoiding the workout would now require more willpower than simply going for a run.

"It totally worked," Michael says. "That simple change got me back to training four days a week." His mileage and stamina grew, and he was ready on race day. He had not found some hidden reserve of grit to get through the 13.1 miles. Instead, he moved the daily decision to run out of his brain's executive function to his subconscious. He automated himself.

That's just one example of what you can accomplish through self-automation. When you tap into this hidden brainpower, there's a host of benefits.

Mental Energy

Researchers estimate the average person makes some 35,000 decisions every single day. It begins when you decide whether or not to hit the snooze button, continues through your choices of breakfast food, which clothes to wear, and if you have time to throw in a load of laundry. You make scores of these little decisions before you ever leave the house.

Once you're out in the world, decisions multiply by the thousands.

The daily overload on your executive function leaves you exhausted. By the end of the day, you have no energy for even the smallest decisions, like what to eat or what TV program to watch. This is a symptom of what social psychologist Roy F. Baumeister termed *decision fatigue.* A wealth of research shows that the more decisions you make, the less energy you have to make good decisions as the day wears on. (While some experts have challenged this claim, because their own experiments failed to duplicate Baumesiter's findings, Baumeister has noted that their methodology was not the same. And most business professionals can affirm the reality of decision fatigue from their own experience.) Your prefrontal cortex burns a lot of fuel. It occupies only about 5 percent of the space in your brain, but it burns about 25 percent of your brain's total energy.

By reducing as much daily decision making through self-automation as possible, you can drastically reduce the number of choices you make in any given day. This frees your mind and reduces stress. It also frees up a lot of brainpower for other, more important things.

Billionaire investor and globetrotter Richard Branson wears the same brand of jeans and a white shirt every day because it simplifies packing. Facebook founder Mark Zuckerberg explained his preference for gray T-shirts, saying, "I really want to clear my life to make it so that I have to make as few decisions as possible about anything except how to best serve this community." Matilda Kahl, head of creative at Sony Entertainment, wore the same white shirt and black pants combination every day for four years. She said, "I did it because I realized how much time and energy I could save during my workdays by just taking out the clothing aspect."

Automate routine choices, and you'll reduce your stress level and gain mental energy.

Problem Solving and Creativity

Have you ever had a breakthrough in your thinking while in the shower? If so, you're not alone. According to cognitive scientist Scott Barry Kaufman, 72 percent of people get creative ideas there. He said, "We did a multinational study and found that people reported more creative inspiration in their showers than they did at work."

That's partly because the shower is already a self-automated environment. Turning on the water, shampooing your hair, bathing yourself—these things involve little or no conscious thought. The active part of your brain is now free to think about something else. Add the state of relaxation you experience in a hot shower, and it's a ready-made idea lab.

A shower takes just a few minutes of your day. Imagine what's possible when you automate more and more decisions and actions. You gain more and more headspace, literally, for creative thought. You will have more freedom to think, ponder problems and ideas, and make connections you hadn't seen before. And the best part? It happens automatically.

Reclaimed Time

Ask anyone how they're doing these days, and you're likely to hear, "Crazy busy!" Yet many of the tasks that contribute to that frazzled feeling of busyness could be managed with much less attention and zero stress through self-automation.

For example, think of the time and energy that goes into daily meal planning, coordinating school and sports schedules, routine household maintenance, or arguments over whose turn it is to take out the trash. Those tasks, and many more, are ripe for self-automation. What if you never again had to:

- Go to the pharmacy to pick up medication
- Remember to order a furnace filter
- Check to see whether you're out of olive oil, laundry soap, or pet food
- Go online and pay your utility bills
- Decide whose turn it is to do the dishes

The list could go on for pages, but you get the point. Many of the small daily choices you make can put on autopilot. Subscription services, auto drafts of recurring payments, menu planning templates, and the like can significantly reduce your daily decision making. While no single instance of automation produces a huge benefit, taken together they save hours each week. Self-automation means making a decision one time rather than 365 times a year. Each bit of time saved adds to the margin you have for the things that matter most.

Greater Productivity

Studies show that roughly 40 percent of our daily activities are done automatically. This goes far beyond basic functions like breathing and heart rate. Actions like turning right out of the driveway when you head for work, scraping the remaining food on your dishes into the trash, or reaching for the remote control from the same spot each time are regulated by a part of your brain called the *basal ganglia.* You choose to do an action once, and, before long, your subconscious takes over and it happens automatically. It takes no willpower to open the fridge when you walk into the kitchen, and willpower alone is usually ineffective at stopping you.

Some automated behaviors may support your productivity, but others undercut it. Checking social media every time you pick up your phone or responding to email whenever you receive a notification are self-automated actions. But they make you less productive, not more. When it comes to productivity, self-automation can make you or break you.

That makes productivity the area where you could see the most immediate benefit of self-automation. As you leverage more complex forms of self-automation (like the rituals we'll see in Level 2), you'll gain focus-building behaviors and eradicate focus killers. You'll routinely find yourself engrossed in high-leverage work, and the interruptions and distractions that plague you now will disappear.

Improved Well-being

In 1972, psychologist Walter Mischel of Stanford

University conducted an experiment in delayed gratification with preschool children. Each child was offered a choice between eating one marshmallow (or pretzel stick, if that's what the child preferred) immediately or having two later. The catch was that the child would have to sit alone in the room with the first treat for fifteen minutes. If they could resist eating it, they'd be rewarded with the second one. This Marshmallow Test has been replicated a number of times and even recently resurfaced, recorded on social media with hilarious results.

Follow-up studies on the original children revealed that those who were able to wait longer for their reward tended to have better test scores, higher educational achievement, and a lower body mass index. The study is often used to suggest that people who have greater willpower will be more successful in life.

Actually, it proves the opposite. The study's authors noted that the kids who resisted the first marshmallow did not rely on willpower. Instead, they did everything possible to forget it existed. They made up songs, hid their faces, or stomped their feet. One little girl even rested her head on the table and fell asleep. These kids weren't mastering temptation by force of will. They were removing themselves, psychologically at least, from the source of desire. We can imagine that these same kids, in later years, didn't have to labor over the choice between watching television and doing homework. They just went to the library.

What does this have to do with self-automation? Everything. According to psychologist Wendy Wood, the reason people who appear to have greater self-control enjoy greater well-being is simple: "They have good habits." They don't battle their desires. They sidestep them. In case after case, she found that those who were able to exercise more consistently, eat healthier snacks, or get adequate sleep all had routinized their behavior. "They didn't have to think about it," she said. "They just did it."

You Can

Self-automation is the key to mastering behaviors you've repeatedly tried and failed to crack through sheer willpower. That's what Michael did with running. And you can do the same with activities that support your desire for good health, better relationships, improved productivity, financial security, or any life domain you choose.

Imagine what your life would be like if you never had to force yourself to focus on work, you just did it. What if you didn't have to muster up the willpower to exercise, or cook, or read, or spend time with family and friends? What if you were able to order all of those activities, in fact most of every day, without conscious thought? You'd be more productive, more connected, healthier, and probably better off financially than ever before. That's what self-automation can do for you. And your first step to harnessing that amazing force is to master the five basic elements of habit formation.

MOMENTUM BUILDER

Picture Success

In the last chapter, you wrote about the problem you're facing. Now describe success in your own words. List at least five things you'd like to be true in your life when this journey is complete. If you'd like, expand the list to a paragraph. What is your vision for your future?

3

How to Form a Habit

Habits are the basic building block of self-automation. To form or break a habit, you must master the four elements of the habit loop.

After completing the Music City Marathon, Michael was on a fitness high. He continued running a couple times a week and didn't need to lay out his running clothes the night before anymore. He recalls, "I was in the best shape of my life, and it felt great!"

The next year, his daughter Megan asked Michael if he'd like to take part in a charity run she was organizing, another half-marathon. Michael eagerly signed on. After all, he'd crushed the last half-marathon. He was sure there'd be no problem with repeating the performance. Though his weekly mileage was down a bit, Michael was confident he could whip himself back into shape in no time.

Then reality hit. The more Michael ran, the more it felt like work. He had far less enthusiasm for this race than the last one, and his training was often interrupted by travel. As the half-marathon drew near, he decided to withdraw. He called Megan and gave her the news. "I was a bit relieved," he said. "But I couldn't figure out what went wrong. I did this once. Why couldn't I do it again?"

Why Habits Fail

The answer was simple: Michael had broken the habit of daily running without realizing it. In his mind, he was still a runner. But he ran only occasionally, not habitually. He'd accidentally automated his running during the prior year, and he'd broken the habit by accident, too.

Most people have a similar experience at some point. We establish a habit—or what we think is a habit—and believe that behavior is on autopilot. It could be anything from making five sales calls a day to reading for an hour each evening to having a date night once a week. These are positive choices that we want to repeat, and we're delighted when they seem to come automatically. Then, often as not, those habits slip away as quickly as they appeared. It's totally frustrating.

In most cases, however, the action was never a habit to begin with. The essence of self-automation is to take certain decisions and behaviors out of your conscious control and hand them over to your subconscious. Unless you have a solid understanding of how that happens, you'll never truly automate the behavior, at least not intentionally.

Research into neuroscience and psychology has identified a clear process by which your subconscious assumes responsibility for certain behaviors. It's called the *habit loop.* And it operates all the time, whether you're aware of it or not. For example, you don't make a decision to reach for your toothbrush every morning. Sure, you had to at the start. But before long, the behavior became a habit. That's the beauty of self-automation. It doesn't take much effort to establish a habit. Your brain will do it for you. But only if all elements of the habit loop are present.

If you want to intentionally form a habit, you need to understand this subconscious process.

When you master the habit loop, you can fully automate just about any decision, action, or behavior you choose.

The Habit Loop

There are four elements in the habit loop. In the year between Michael's half-marathon experiences, he managed to snip the loop in each of those four places. Not surprisingly, the habit disappeared. Let's take a close look at these four elements: *activation trigger*, *response*, *reward*, and *repetition*. When we're done, you'll understand how a habit is formed, and how to make it work for you.

Activation Trigger

Most people think repetition alone is the key to establishing a habit. While repetition is important, it's not the only element in the habit loop—and it's not the first one. In a perfect world, Michael would have laced up his training shoes every morning and gone for a run. But the world is not perfect. He faced countless distractions and interruptions. Your repetition of any action is bound to be interrupted by life's circumstances, just like Michael's. To get an action firmly embedded in your subconscious, you need something that keeps bringing you back to it. That something is called an *activation trigger* (or "cue").

An activation trigger can be any circumstance that elicits a response from you. In Michael's case, it was tripping over his running gear on the way to the bathroom. That was the cue that both reminded him of his desire to run and prompted him to take action. When he thought his habit was fully automated and quit laying out his running gear each evening, he cut the activation trigger out of his habit loop. Not surprisingly, his running frequency declined.

Think about any habit you currently have. I'll bet you can identify the activation trigger for that

ACTIVATION TRIGGER		RESPONSE
Turn on your computer	▶	Check email
The time is noon	▶	Open the refrigerator
Hear a *ding*!	▶	Pick up your cell phone
Arrive home on Friday	▶	Reach for a drink or a snack
Pull out of the driveway	▶	Turn in the direction of work

habitual action. Here are few of the more common activation triggers and responses.

Whether you are aware of it or not, every habitual action is preceded by an activation trigger. Looking more closely at this phenomenon, researchers have identified several kinds of activation triggers that can initiate a response. These include the time of day, your location, a preceding event, your emotional state, even the presence of a particular person or group of people. This explains why you may feel anxious when you enter a dentist's office, or when you walk into your own kitchen, you feel hunger. Location is the activation trigger. And it's why you may reach for a bag of chips every time you feel angry, lonely, tired, or bored. Your emotional state can be a powerful trigger.

To establish a productive habit, it's vital to pair it with an activation trigger. What do you want to do without further thought? That's the response you're trying to automate. Once you identify it, you can find an activation trigger to prompt action. That could be as simple as doing it at the same time every day (like first thing in the morning), or in the same place (such as at your desk), or after finishing another action (perhaps after supper).

Not surprisingly, one of the easiest ways to break a habit is to decouple it from its activation trigger. If you want to quit checking messages by habit every time you look at your phone, start leaving your phone in a drawer. If you want to stop the habit of complaining, avoid being with the people to whom you complain. Get rid of the negative activation trigger, and the response will die on its own.

What about an automated activation trigger, like a calendar reminder or an alarm? Those can be helpful for getting started. But in the long run, it's best to choose one of the triggers mentioned above. Studies have shown that using an alarm makes a habit easier to initiate but harder to maintain. Use a more natural activation trigger if you can.

Response

The response is the behavior you want to automate. These are generally things you will want to do every day, or perhaps every week, without making a conscious choice. This is another mistake Michael made with his running habit. He subtly altered the response. Rather than running on particular days of the week, Michael admitted to only running whenever he remembered to. The activation trigger was gone, the response was variable, and the habit died.

Here are some ideal candidates for self-automation, listed by category:

HEALTH

- Daily grooming
- Haircuts/hairstyling
- Medication
- Exercise
- Food choices
- Recurring health appointments
- Prescription refills

BUSINESS

- Responding to messages
- Scheduling meetings
- Tracking expenses
- Focused time for deep work
- Reviewing reports
- Sales calls

HOUSEHOLD MANAGEMENT

- Budgeting
- Household chores
- Bill payment
- Buying gasoline and auto maintenance

- Lawncare
- Grocery shopping

RELATIONSHIPS

- Daily debriefing with family members
- Date nights
- Girls or guys night out
- Playdates
- Entertaining

REJUVENATION

- Scheduling time away from work
- Hobbies
- Bedtime
- Screen time
- Reading

What makes a good target for self-automation? Any decision or action about which you can answer yes to these two questions:

1. Is this something I want to do consistently without further thought or consideration?
2. Can I pair this with an activation trigger so that I'll be prompted to do it?

If so, you can build a habit to support this action.

We have one more tip. Sometimes you can outsource the action to a computer rather than to your subconscious. Online auto bill payment, automated reordering of household supplies, auto-refilling of prescriptions, automatic deposits to savings accounts: these are just a few ways that a computer can take over self-automated tasks.

Reward

Michael was genuinely puzzled when he couldn't motivate himself to train for his second half-marathon. It was essentially the same challenge: run 13.1 miles. But this time he was running for a different reason. The first time around, he wanted to get in better shape and set a good example for his team. He also liked the idea of taking on a new challenge. As it turns out, those were strong motivators that provided the promise of a reward. His desire to get in better shape and achieve a goal were powerful *intrinsic* motivators. His desire to lead his team and not go back on his word to them was a powerful *extrinsic* motivator. He stood to gain better health, a sense of achievement, and recognition for being a good leader.

This time, none of those reasons were in play. He was already in pretty good shape. He'd already proven to himself that he could run 13.1 miles. And he hadn't announced his intention publicly, so there was no external pressure. In short, the reward to be gained from this run was not sufficient to sustain motivation.

Behavioral scientists, starting with Ivan Pavlov in the nineteenth century, are aware of the relationship between reward and repeated behavior. Pavlov was able to prove that by ringing a bell while feeding dogs, he could eventually make the dogs salivate without food just by ringing the bell. The activation trigger (bell) produced a response (salivation) in expectation of a reward (food). In terms of habit formation, we haven't changed a bit since the 1890s. Habit formation is inextricably linked to the prospect of reward.

Below are some rewards you may be receiving for automated behaviors, even though you're unaware of it. Notice that some of these rewards are intrinsic and some are extrinsic, some are positive and some negative.

To fully automate a behavior, it must offer some reward. That might be as simple as enjoying your first cup of coffee only after letting the dog out. Or it could be more complex, as was Michael's desire to both lead his team by training and avoid embarrassment by failing to run the half-marathon. To

RESPONSE		REWARD
Constantly checking messages	▶	Affirmation from colleagues
Running	▶	Endorphin high
Complaining about workload	▶	Affirmation from peers
Over-formatting spreadsheets	▶	Satisfies internal need for order
Ordering the same meal at lunch	▶	Reduces stress of decision making
Completing a sales report on time	▶	Avoid being publicly reminded
Filing expense report on time	▶	Avoid reminder from accounting
Take out the trash every week	▶	Avoid conflict with housemates

establish a habit, be sure that your desired response holds some benefit to you. And be explicit in stating, at least to yourself, what that benefit is.

To break a habit, scuttle the reward. For example, if you want to quit checking social media frequently, shut off the audio notification so there's no endorphin rush from hearing the sound. By removing that tiny reward, you begin to extinguish the behavior.

Repetition

How long does it take to install a habit? You'll hear a variety of answers to that question. Some will say six weeks, some a month, and some say just three weeks. There are a lot of opinions, and that's just what most of them are: opinions.

Psychological research indicates that it takes much longer to install a habit than most people realize. And the length of time varies by the type of behavior. To install a habit around healthy drinking choices requires an average of fifty-nine days. To make a healthy eating habit takes longer, an average of sixty-five days. For exercise, it's longer still, averaging ninety-one days. So, when you begin to automate a behavior, give yourself time. You'll need sixty to ninety days of repetition before the behavior is truly automatic. That was another error Michael made in training. He didn't repeat the pattern long enough for it to become a true habit.

Don't be discouraged by those numbers. Consistency is not the only goal in habit formation. If you miss a day, don't beat yourself up. That'll only make you more likely to miss another day. Instead, get right back at it the next day. Even when the action is something difficult or tedious, it really does get easier with time.

Time to Build

A day or two after Michael told Megan he was dropping out of the half-marathon, she called him back. "Dad, I think you should reconsider. Although you didn't announce this to your whole team, a lot of people know that you planned to run. I really think it will ding your credibility to drop out now."

"I knew she was right," Michael said. "That reminder was just the motivation I needed to get back on track." There's the power of a solid extrinsic motivator showing itself again. Michael didn't want to let others down. He was running for his own sense of integrity. With that reward in place, he was able to reinstall his activation trigger, get back to running, and complete the loop with repetition. He did compete in the charity event, and he even bettered his time!

Think about what would be possible for you if you could form a habit at-will rather than by accident. How freeing would it be if you could finally gain consistency in your self-care, personal finances, household management, and personal interactions? How would it feel to focus deeply on your work during the day, then be fully present with family or friends and never have that nagging feeling that you're forgetting something important?

Master the habit loop of activation trigger, response, reward, and repetition. With these basic tools, you can start to design the life you truly want to live.

MOMENTUM BUILDER

Habit Goal Template

Let's begin your transformation by designing your first intentional habit. When installing new habits, concentrate on one at a time to avoid being overwhelmed. Give each one time to succeed. Choose the first behavior you'd like to automate, then determine the following elements. Write the habit goal in the goal detail pages of your Full Focus Planner, or anywhere you can refer to it daily.

When setting a habit goal, think through the:

- Key Motivations (3 reasons this matters to you)
- Activation Trigger (to cue the behavior)
- Response (the behavior you want to automate)

- Reward (state the reward and whether it is intrinsic, extrinsic, or both)
- Repetition (start date, stop date, and frequency)
- Tracking (state how you will monitor your progress)

SELF-AUTOMATION

LEVEL 2

Leverage Rituals to Automate Multiple Tasks

4

How Rituals Set You Up for Success

Rituals are habit chains that multiply the power of a simple habit. Set each day up for success with four Daily Rituals.

Megan is what we call a Quick Start. That term comes from the Kolbe A Index, an instrument we use frequently at Michael Hyatt & Co. to understand how people naturally approach a task. Quick Starts tend to, well, start quickly. They love to dive headlong into a project and figure out the details as they go. So, it's not surprising that Quick Starts sometimes bite off a little more work than they can chew. That's exactly what happened to Megan on the day before school started last year.

The Miller clan, Megan, Joel, and their five children, had arrived home late one evening from a weekend at the lake. Jonah was set to start homeschooling in two days. The following morning, Megan created a to-do list. These were items that absolutely had to be accomplished before the start of school. She had one day to do them. There were fourteen items on the list, ranging from sublimely simple, like "Print homework charts,"—to the impossibly complex, like "Write a training plan for baby Naomi's new nanny," who was to start work the following day.

"There was easily a week's worth of work on that list," Megan said, "but I somehow thought I could get it done in one afternoon." In true Quick Start fashion, she started with the first and seemingly simplest task on the list: "Clean the kitchen." It seemed like an easy way to get started and build momentum.

Not so much. Cleaning the fridge led to disinfecting the trash can, then washing down the cupboards, dusting the woodwork, scouring the sink, and cleaning the oven. "After eight hours, I was exhausted," Megan said. "I'd spent the whole day cleaning and felt like I hadn't accomplished anything." Meanwhile, Jonah's lesson plan wasn't ready, the garage still needed tidying, and there was still no plan for training the new nanny, who would arrive in ten hours. "I was a basket case," Megan said. "When Joel found me on the tile floor, cleaning the grout with a toothbrush and listing all the reasons I couldn't manage my home or my life, he held a mini-intervention."

"Just go to bed, darlin," he said. "It'll all be okay in the morning." Joel was right, of course. Megan returned to her task list first thing after breakfast. As if by magic, solutions to the tangle of tasks presented themselves. A few were accomplished in just a few minutes. Others were deferred or delegated. One or two were dropped altogether.

Problems that seem impossible late in the day may be easily solved with morning energy, or vice versa.

Yet there's more at stake here than efficient use of time. By taking on important tasks when her energy was low, Megan did more than waste an afternoon. "I sabotaged my effectiveness *and* missed out on some things that are really important to me," she recalled. As a Quick Starter, Megan enjoys tackling things as they come, but she always holds sacred:

- Spending the evening with family.
- Going to bed at a decent hour to get quality sleep in order tackle the next day.
- Taking a morning walk to appreciate nature and the beauty of a new day.
- Spending time just by herself for some personal rejuvenation before the start of a busy week.
- Having all-day energy, from morning to afternoon to evening.

In the quest for productivity, most of us pack our days chock full of tasks. We think we will get more done by working longer and harder. That seldom works. The energy it takes to power through a tough task usually robs energy from more important but less urgent activities. And the tax on our mental and physical bandwidth cascades through our emotional lives like a bowling ball.

To be fully productive, you must structure your day to focus your best energy on your most important work without sacrificing the rest, rejuvenation, and relationships you need to remain effective. The best way to create that structure is to automate the front and back of your day with daily rituals.

Super Habits to the Rescue

A *ritual* is "any practice or pattern of behavior regularly performed in a set manner." For example, most professional athletes have a pregame ritual, a series of actions that set them up mentally and physically to perform at their best. This is true of high achievers across all professions. Mason Currey's book *Daily Rituals: How Artists Work* explores the daily rituals of more than one hundred fifty novelists, poets, playwrights, painters, philosophers, scientists, mathematicians, and others. Rituals help these diverse professionals achieve more by doing less. Your daily rituals, says Currey, "can be a finely calibrated mechanism for taking advantage of a range of limited resources: time (the most limited resource of all) as well as willpower, self-discipline, optimism."

Close up, a ritual is a daisy chain of self-automation. Activated by a single trigger, this sequence of habits spins through all the activities needed to create a productive day, such as self-care or teeing up your first major task. It ensures that you accomplish the right things at the best possible time, so you're perfectly positioned for high-leverage work. Daily rituals are like the pilings on a pier or the footers for a building. They provide for the foundation to be built. Here are four ways daily rituals set you up for success.

Improved Creativity

Some people think rituals stifle creativity. In fact, it's just the opposite. It takes a good deal of creativity to design an effective ritual. But once implemented, it demands little or no conscious thought. Rather than designing a new solution every time you encounter a problem, you create a ritual. As a result, you're applying the same solution every time. This frees up a great deal of mental bandwidth and lets you focus your creativity on new projects.

For example, think about driving to your office or some other place you routinely visit. The first time you go, you have to think about how to get there. You choose the best route. You may experiment a few times to see which route is most efficient. But after becoming familiar with the route, you never think consciously about it again. You turn the same direction every time, automatically. Your mind is free to think about other things.

Consistent Self-Care

Daily rituals ensure that you don't skip small but important actions. They automate things like exercise, proper eating, self-awareness practices like journaling or meditation, and adequate sleep.

Pressing deadlines can steamroll anything that's not urgent. Your rituals keep you grounded, no matter how hectic your life may be.

Increased Efficiency

Once installed, a ritual happens automatically. Within a short time you don't have to think about what to do next. As an example, the moment you clear out your inbox as the first step of your ritual, you proceed to the second step, which is opening your calendar. There's no time spent decision making or task switching. Muscle memory moves you from one task to the next, picking up momentum as you go.

Continuous Improvement

Rituals are self-correcting over time. When you install a new ritual, there will probably be a few snags early on. You'll realize something vital you've left out, or you may discover that certain tasks just don't flow because they're in the wrong order. Because rituals take on the power of habit, they can easily be corrected. You simply add a step or rearrange the order. After a bit of repetition, the changes are assimilated into the ritual, and you keep building momentum. The ritual becomes more and more effective over time. But remember the potential traps—clip any of the four elements of the habit loop and you'll be back to square one before you know it.

Four Pillars of a Productive Day

At Michael Hyatt & Co., we use and recommend four foundational rituals: morning, evening, workday startup, and workday shutdown. These rituals will set you up for success every day, regardless of what the week may bring. You'll move predictably and efficiently into your workday, which conserves your mental bandwidth and helps you focus. And with an evening ritual, each day will end with a sense of calm and confidence, which sets you up for success both at home and at work the next day. We've listed some typical elements of these Daily Rituals below. Yours may turn out to be quite different, but this will show you how rituals support your work and well-being day in and day out.

Morning Ritual

The Morning Ritual starts the moment you wake up and carries you all the way into the office. Here are some typical elements:

- Make a cup of coffee
- Read inspirational literature or meditate
- Journal
- Review personal goals
- Exercise
- Check in with your spouse
- Prepare children for school or childcare

When you perform the same way, in the same order, every day, it makes your mornings consistent and ensures that you don't forget any small but important actions. This ensures that you arrive for work feeling rested and ready for the day. The order of your routine is personal, but whatever order you decide, stick to it.

If you live alone or do not have children in your home, you may be able to devote a couple of hours to a morning ritual. If you're in a different life stage, you may have considerably less time. That's okay. Even fifteen minutes, used intentionally, is enough to get your day started right.

Workday Startup

The Workday Startup Ritual kicks in as soon as you

arrive for work. By repeating the same actions in the same order every day, muscle memory will do most of the work for you. You can quickly and efficiently move through a small set of tasks you need to do at the start of each day. Again, the list and order of elements will vary by person, but there are some typical items:

- Turn on your computer and open the apps you need for this ritual
- Empty your email inbox
- Catch up on chat messages (using Slack, Teams, or other messaging platform)
- Check social media
- Review your Weekly Big 3 (which we'll discuss in chapter 6)
- Review your schedule
- Transfer to-do items and appointments to your Full Focus Planner

We recommend allowing thirty minutes for this ritual. Make it a calendar appointment with yourself each day. This keeps you from dragging these tasks through the entire morning, sabotaging your focus.

When you've completed everything, your mind will be clear of any nagging thoughts about upcoming tasks or outstanding messages. You'll be focused and ready to dive in on deep work.

Workday Shutdown

The Workday Shutdown Ritual is a bookend for the Startup Ritual. Allow about half an hour for this at the close of your workday. That means concluding meetings or other tasks thirty minutes before you plan to leave the office. This ritual will likely be similar to your Startup Ritual. Common shutdown activities include:

- Empty your email inbox
- Check chat and phone messages
- List your wins
- Review your calendar for the next day
- Transfer unfinished tasks back into your task management system
- Choose your Daily Big 3 tasks for the following day (more on this in chapter 6).
- Tidy your workspace

- Close all apps and shutdown your computer
- Turn off the lights

This ritual allows you to walk out the door with a sense of accomplishment for what you were able to achieve that day, and the confidence that comes from having a solid plan in place for the next day. You can take your mind off work and relax.

Evening Ritual

The Evening Ritual is one of the most overlooked parts of the day for many people. Just as the Morning Ritual prepares you to face the day, the Evening Ritual prepares your mind and body for restful sleep. The elements of an Evening Ritual can vary by individual, but can consist of:

- Turning off all screens one hour before bedtime
- Laying out clothes for the following day
- Prepping meals for the following day
- Reviewing children's schedules
- Reading
- Sharing your wins with a spouse, family member, or friend

The Evening Ritual allows you to feel both ready for the next day and grateful for the one ending. It relaxes your mind and body so that you fall asleep easily. Whatever items you build into this ritual, they should accomplish setting you up for a good night's rest, so you can face the next day with full vigor.

Automated Self-Discipline

When anyone at Michael Hyatt and Co. describes their daily rituals to people, they often have the same reaction, "Wow, you're the most disciplined person I know." We know that's not true, of course. We've all simply made intentional choices about the daily actions that will make us successful over the long haul. Then, we automated them with rituals. We'll be the first to admit we don't complete all our rituals 100 percent of the time. Life's too unpredictable for that. But we do them roughly 90 percent of the time, and that has laid a solid foundation for growth in both our professional and personal lives.

You can do the same. Daily rituals do not require heaps of self-discipline. They're simply a string of habits that you place together. And like all habits, they run automatically once installed well. What will set you up for success each day? The answer to that question will form your own daily rituals.

MOMENTUM BUILDER

Choose Outcomes for Your Daily Rituals

To create a Daily Ritual, begin with the end in mind. How do you want to feel at the beginning of each day? What do you want to be true at the end of each workday? The answers to questions like these give you a target to shoot for. For now, draw a mental picture of the outcome of each ritual. You can do that by answering the following questions. In the next chapter, you'll learn how to construct a ritual to meet that goal.

- How do you want to feel when you leave for work each day?
- What would help you to feel that way?
- Describe how you'd like to enter each workday. What would have to be true for you to achieve that?
- What would you need to do to ensure that you leave work in a relaxed state, knowing you haven't forgotten anything vital?
- How much sleep do you want to have each night? What needs to happen for you to get that rest?

5

Taking Daily Rituals to the Next Level

You have daily rituals, whether you are aware of it or not. When you intentionally optimize those rituals, you multiply their effectiveness.

Our founder, Michael, is an enthusiastic early adopter of new technologies. He's been using personal computers since Compaq introduced its Portable in 1983. "I actually bought one of the original run of 53,000 machines," Michael said. "I was working in sales at the time, but I paid for it out of my own pocket."

That's because Michael was traveling thousands of miles a month, visiting customers for a large publishing company. Orders had to be handwritten on the road, then transcribed once back at the office. Although the "Portable" weighed a whopping twenty-eight pounds, it saved hours of time each week, which added up to hundreds of hours per year.

Though it seems laughable now, that clunky machine with its 5 ¼-inch floppy drive, 9-inch green screen, and paltry 128K memory was like a miracle. It took the work Michael was already doing, streamlined it, simplified it, and freed him to concentrate on selling more books.

The very next year, Apple introduced the Macintosh. Though now a devoted Apple user, Michael was not initially sold on the brand. With its graphical user interface and mouse, the Macintosh was certainly easy to use. "It just seemed more like a novelty," Michael recalls, "but I did buy one for a client."

Here's how it happened. Michael was working with an author who was resistant to change, to put it mildly. He wrote his books longhand on yellow legal pads. Then the author edited them by cutting and pasting sections into a massive scroll. It was tedious and time consuming both for the author and the publishing house. Yet, the author's books were always a hot seller, so Michael was eager to keep the relationship going.

Michael flew to meet the author in the mountains of New Mexico, where he was working on his latest book. Michael brought along a brand new Macintosh and showed him how easy it was to use and how much time it could save. For two hours, the author listened patiently. "I wound up my pitch with a big finish," Michael recalls. "I said, 'This will take the work you're already doing, streamline it, simplify it, and free you to focus on other priorities.'"

The writer was not impressed. "You expect me to learn all that?" he asked. "No thanks." And with that, he picked up his yellow pad and went back to work.

"I couldn't believe it," Michael later said. "Why would anybody stick with a clunky, time-consuming system when they could accomplish twice the work in half the time?"

Of course, people do this all the time. And not just with technology. Everyone already has a morning routine and an evening routine, and a workday startup order and a shutdown ritual. Most people are simply unaware of them. They never stop to notice what they're doing, how long it takes, and whether it serves them well. Sometimes their rituals actually undercut their success, yet they stick with them anyway. With a little intentionality, you can upgrade your Daily Rituals to accomplish more by doing less.

Making Rituals Work for You

The biggest reason people are resistant to changing their rituals is because there is a cost to every change. Like moving from analog to digital, installing a solid ritual requires a bit of time, some learning, and even trial and error. It requires us to be honest about what's working and what isn't. And it means pushing ourselves to change some comfortable habits that have outlived their usefulness.

But it's worth it. The time you spend to install solid rituals at the front and back of your day will pay dividends in margin and focus for years to come. And it's far less daunting than it may seem. You can install and optimize any daily ritual in just four simple steps. Master these, and you'll never again wonder, "Why is it so hard to get out the door in the morning?"

Document Your Current Rituals

We naturally develop habits around four daily time slots: morning, evening, workday startup, and workday shutdown. Most are formed unintentionally and are therefore invisible to us. Remember, the habit loop is always working. We form habits all the time. But we need them to work for us, not against us.

The place to start in installing any routine is to notice what you are already doing in that area. For the four daily routines, ask yourself these questions:

- What's the first thing I do when I wake up? What do I do after that?
- What do I do first when I start work? Then what? Then what?
- What do I do once I've decided to stop working for the day? Then what?
- What's the last thing I do before I fall asleep? What comes before that? And before that?

You can probably reconstruct these routines from memory. If not, just pay attention to what you do the rest of today and tomorrow. Write out the steps, in order, and jot down the approximate time each action takes.

Evaluate Your Rituals

To produce intentional change, always start with the end and work your way back. This is what you did in the Ritual Targets Worksheet from chapter 4. Here are some examples for each of the four Daily Rituals. Your targets may vary, but it'll give you the idea.

AFTER MY MORNING RITUAL, I WANT TO FEEL:

- Prepared
- Eager
- Confident

AFTER MY WORKDAY STARTUP RITUAL, I WANT TO FEEL:

- Focused
- In control
- Calm

AFTER MY WORKDAY SHUTDOWN RITUAL, I WANT TO FEEL:

- Finished
- Released
- Relaxed

AFTER MY EVENING RITUAL, I WANT TO FEEL:

- Accomplished
- Important
- At peace

Your rituals aren't simply a few mundane actions to get out of the way. They gather vital tasks that you want to routinize (self-automate) to ensure they happen daily. In the case of the four Daily Rituals, each one should set you up for success in the next phase of your day. Review your existing rituals through the lens of your target outcomes. Ask, "Do these rituals work?" and "Are they accomplishing their stated purpose?" If so, great! No change is needed. If they're not working, you have more work to do.

You need to discover why the ritual is not producing its intended outcome. When a ritual doesn't work, it's usually for one of three reasons.

Something's Missing. When a habit is missing from your ritual, one of your key needs will be unmet. For example, you might not have an activity to prepare you for rest, so you have trouble falling asleep. Or you're not checking messages at Workday Startup, giving you the feeling of being out of the loop all morning long.

Something's Changed. This may result from a life change, job change, or a change in your goals. For example, you may start working from home, where, suddenly, you have no "unwind time" to transition from work to home. Or you added a fitness goal but didn't add time to your morning ritual.

Something Doesn't Fit. There may be a habit in place that actually works against your purpose. For example, you're checking social media first thing in the morning, so you don't have enough time for your full morning ritual. Or you're scheduling meetings right up to quitting time, giving you no time for workday shutdown.

Once you have visibility into the problem, you can address it. You are in control of your time. The way you begin and end your day is totally up to you. You can change your habits to better serve the ends you want to accomplish.

Re-Engineer Your Rituals for Success

Based on your findings from examining your rituals, optimize them to produce your intended results. Remember that rituals are not about self-discipline; they're about self-automation. The point here is not disciplining yourself to do things you don't really want to do. The idea is to organize the activities that set you up for success in such a way that they happen automatically. We have some principles to keep in mind as you get started.

Rituals take time. One of the most common reasons rituals fail is that we try to do too much in too little time. None of us has unlimited time, so carefully select the habits to include based on your available time. That will vary depending on your stage of life. You may not have time for a two-hour morning routine, and that's okay. Find habits you can reasonably accomplish given whatever season of life you're in now.

Rituals require an activation trigger. Every habit needs one, and a ritual is a chain of habits. Setting the activation trigger for the beginning of the ritual is critical (see chapter 3). After that, the completion of one activity will serve as the activation trigger for the next.

Rituals dislike friction. Rituals don't fail because you lack willpower, but they can be derailed by friction. Pay careful attention to the sequencing of your rituals to avoid getting sidetracked or slowed down. For example, I find it best to close all apps on my computer during my Workday Shutdown. That way, I'm not distracted by open windows or unfinished documents during my Workday Startup the next day.

Iterate

When you've arranged your rituals as best you can, it's finally time to implement them. But remember that rituals are always a work in progress. If something doesn't work, it doesn't mean you've failed.

You've simply discovered a better way to organize your activities—which is a big win! Reorder them and begin again.

Even when a ritual is running smoothly, it's important to review it at least quarterly. Just follow these steps again. Remember, you are building them toward the outcome you want. How do you want to feel at the beginning of the day? At the end of your workday? If your rituals aren't getting you there, optimize them until they do.

Imagine the Freedom

The author we mentioned earlier that Michael worked with eventually did begin using a computer. He also went on to write several more best-selling books. We can't help but wonder how much greater his impact might have been if he'd seen the value of streamlining his process earlier. In the same way, you may be clunking through your day, not realizing how much mental bandwidth and time you're wasting by rituals that simply don't work. Imagine how much more productive you would be if you sailed through each morning without being bogged down by the thousand little choices that must be made to get you up, at work, and started on your first major task? How pleasant and rejuvenating would your evenings be if you could finish working at a predictable time, feeling relaxed and fully present for your family or personal interests?

Remember, you already have Daily Routines. If you're not beginning and ending each day with a sense of calm and confidence, it simply means those routines are not working for you. With a little intentionality, you can streamline the work you're already doing, simplify it, optimize it, and become free to focus on the things that matter most.

MOMENTUM BUILDER

Design Your First Daily Ritual

Design your first Daily Ritual by following these steps. If you have a Full Focus Planner, use the Daily Rituals pages for this. If not, write them anywhere you can easily refer to and revise the ritual. Remember to build the ritual toward one of your target outcomes from the Momentum Builder in chapter 4.

First, catalog what you already do. You have some daily ritual already in place, though you may be unaware of it. Start by writing down those activities, in order, and including an estimated time for each one.

Second, identify what works and what doesn't. Critically examine each element of your ritual. Is it helping you reach your desired outcome? Is it detracting? Could it be strengthened? Is anything missing from your list?

Third, reengineer as needed. Remove any items from your list that aren't working. Tweak those that could be more effective. And add any missing items that you need to help you reach your target. Then revise the order as needed, including the time needed.

That's it! You have designed your first Daily Ritual.

6

Using Rituals to Manage Your Energy

In the knowledge economy, energy, not time, is your greatest asset. Continually renew your energy with three Rejuvenation Rituals.

"I used to feel a little guilty about this," Michael told our team. "But I learned to embrace it years ago. I do it every single day if I possibly can." He was talking about the time-honored practice of taking a midday nap.

Michael recounted how his practice of taking a nap in the middle of a workday was sometimes taken for laziness in the corporate world. As he rose through the ranks in the publishing business, he considered giving it up. "I knew how foggy and unfocused I would be without it," Michael said. "But nobody wants to be labeled a slacker." It was a catch-22.

Then he met Sam Moore, who was CEO of Thomas Nelson at the time. Moore admitted to his young protégé that he too was a napper. "Every day after lunch, I lie down on the sofa in my office," Moore said. "I hold my car keys in my right hand and let my hand hang toward the floor. When the car keys fall out of my hand, I know I'm done." Evidently, artist Salvador Dali had a similar practice. He called it "slumber with a key."

Empowered by Sam's advice, Michael kept up his midday ritual of lunch followed by a nap of twenty to thirty minutes. It turns out he was not alone. Leaders and thinkers including Napoleon, Leonardo da Vinci, Thomas Edison, Eleanor Roosevelt, Winston Churchill, and Ronald Reagan all napped as a way to restore energy and make them more alert throughout the day and into the evening.

The fact that this practice has been shared by so many great leaders underscores a key principle of self-management: time is fixed, but energy flexes. To be fully productive, you must manage your energy throughout each day and throughout the week. There's no better way to do this than having a ritual.

Automated Self-Care

During the Industrial Age, we came to think of our bodies as machines. Beginning with Frederick Winslow Taylor, whose ideas started the modern Efficiency Movement, we have believed that the secret to being more productive is to eliminate any wasted effort or supposedly nonproductive activity. That way, we could get more done in less time. The science of efficiency naturally gave rise to the field of time management.

The old approach of managing time and motion is not sufficient in the knowledge economy. We work mostly with our minds, which consume a tremendous amount of energy. Researchers have determined that the brain, which accounts for only 2 percent of an average person's body weight, consumes 20 percent of its energy. So, about 400 of your 2,000-calorie daily intake is used just to keep your brain going.

The bulk of your brain's energy consumption is put toward sustaining your alertness, monitoring your environment, and managing internal functions.

But doing "cognitively challenging" work for 8 hours ups the brain's energy demand by about 100 calories, or up to 25 percent. If an activity is exceptionally demanding for an extended period of time, the tax on your thinking could be as high as using 200 calories and up to 50 percent of your brain's total energy.

In knowledge work, it is more important to manage your energy than your time. Both matter, but energy matters more. This means some things that would have seemed unproductive in the industrial age, like taking a nap, are now vital for maintaining your mental energy. You need to rejuvenate yourself.

Your rejuvenation rituals will be personal to you and your type of work because we all have different chronotypes and constitutions. Even so, there are three essential rituals that nearly everyone needs for managing their energy and productivity.

Midday Rituals

Most people experience an energy dip in the afternoon. According to the Sleep Foundation, this dip occurs between two and four o'clock for most people. Our *circadian rhythm*, which regulates our urge to sleep, takes a predictable dive, our core temperature drops a bit, and we get sleepy. The effect can be worsened by sitting at your desk for a long period of time, certain foods you may have eaten, and being slightly dehydrated. Skipping lunch makes it even worse, as your blood sugar is likely to be lower, robbing your brain of the energy it needs for deep afternoon work.

To counteract that midday slump, you must manage your energy. Since that energy trough is highly consistent, it makes sense to automate your response to it. A solid midday ritual will likely include some, if not all, of these elements:

- A break from work, including leaving your workspace
- Physical movement
- Nutrition and hydration
- Rest, and possibly a nap
- Socializing

For Megan, the Midday Ritual includes lunch and spending time with her children. As a work-from-home mom, a midday nap is hard to come by. "I actually take several brief breaks throughout the day," Megan says. "I spend a little time with the kids, stretch my legs a bit, get away from my computer, and clear my mind. A little bit of rejuvenation goes a long way."

Your midday ritual may differ from Megan's, but we strongly recommend that you design one. As knowledge workers, our effectiveness depends on being alert, not merely present. Consider:

- When you will break from work. A consistent time activation trigger will establish your ritual.
- What you will eat, where, and with whom. We strongly recommend not eating at your desk.
- What types of activities will help rejuvenate you, such as a nap, a walk, a bit of personal reading, or conversation with friends.

Midday rituals make you more productive, increase creativity, and can even improve your health. Automate your midday to avoid the hurdle of making daily decisions about important aspects of your self-care.

Weekend Ritual

Many people, especially business leaders, work almost constantly, even on weekends. A Harvard study of CEOs revealed that leaders worked an average of 9.7 hours per day or 48.5 hours per week. That's already a hefty schedule. But they also worked 79 percent of weekend days for an average of 3.9

hours daily, and 70 percent of vacation days with an average of 2.4 hours on those supposed days off. Altogether, the CEOs worked an average of 62.5 hours a week, with a considerably large chunk on weekends and vacations.

Seeing the need for an off-switch, Michael and Megan established several practices early in the life of our company that help all of us keep work from bleeding into the weekend. It begins with a small change to the Friday Workday Shutdown and then sticking to some firm practices on the weekend.

"On Fridays, I sweep my to-do lists from the preceding week," Michael explains. "I mark each open item so I won't miss it during my Weekly Preview." (More on that to come). This gives him the confidence to leave work for the next two days knowing that no important item will be forgotten.

Also, the lights in our shared workspace at Michael Hyatt & Co. go off automatically at six o'clock on Friday. For anyone still working, that's an activation trigger to shut down for the weekend. Our leadership team follows some version of this Friday Shutdown Ritual. It frees them to focus attention on friends and family, rest, and other interests.

To ensure that we won't slip back into work mode come Saturday, Michael and Megan created some rules for themselves, which have taken on the power of habit and have become company-wide practices. On most weekends, the entire team is able to follow them.

First, we don't work on weekends. There are exceptions, of course. But they're infrequent. For the most part, we're able to get our work done Monday through Friday, leaving weekends completely free. With rare exceptions, there are no work-related emails, texts, or Slack messages on Saturday or Sunday.

Second, we don't think about work on weekends. This habit is triggered by the Friday Shutdown Ritual. Sweeping open tasks clears the mind of urgent items. When every task or project is accounted for, they cannot become activation triggers that put the brain back in work mode.

Third, we don't read about work on weekends. Our team members are lifelong learners. Most are avid consumers of books and podcasts on business and leadership. Setting this rule helps us avoid thinking about work on weekends. We simply read or listen to other material on Saturday and Sunday. The hidden benefit is that by forcing ourselves into other types of content, we trigger imagination and creativity, which improves our productivity during the week.

Finally, we don't talk about work on weekends. "This was really our first rule," Megan said. "Since my dad, my husband, and I all work in the company, we had to set this boundary for our own sanity."

They talk a lot at weekend family gatherings, but never about what's coming up on Monday. Many team members now practice this as well, leaving work-talk between spouses limited to the workweek only. Megan and Michael have been purposeful about instituting the Friday Shutdown Ritual. They know that a company culture starts at the top and they want their entire team to be at their very best.

Your mind and body need a complete break from work every week. When and how you take that is up to you. When you automate your breaks, it will cement rejuvenation practices into your weekly schedule.

Weekly Preview

Have you ever felt a vague sense of dread as the weekend draws to a close? We've all likely felt the "Sunday scaries" on at least one Sunday evening. If so, you're not alone. A survey commissioned by LinkedIn found that 80 percent of working American adults worry about the upcoming workweek on

Sundays. Another survey revealed that the average time of onset for this anxiety is 3:58 p.m.

The reasons for this anxiety seem to be the stress we feel about returning to work, not knowing what awaits us, or not truly enjoying what we do Monday-Friday. As our lives—and weekends—have become busier, we have less time to rest and rejuvenate. It seems that we're not mentally and emotionally prepared to resume work when the alarm rings bright and early Monday morning.

One answer to combat this anxiety is a ritual called the Weekly Preview. Users of the Full Focus Planner will be familiar with the concept. Even if you don't use the Full Focus system yet, you can design your own Weekly Preview to help you enter the week feeling calm and in control.

Some of our leaders conduct their Weekly Preview on Friday afternoons, others on Sunday evenings or Monday mornings. Simply having this practice in place allows your mind to relax. When urgent thoughts pop up on the weekend, you can easily put them to rest, knowing that you'll deal with them during your Weekly Preview. You can be confident that the week ahead is well in hand. The Weekly Preview is made of six parts.

List Your Wins. Put yourself in a positive frame of mind by listing all you accomplished last week. High achievers have no trouble remembering which goals were missed. Listing wins, even small ones, starts you off feeling confident.

Conduct an After-Action Review. This is a no-holds-barred examination of the past week. It should be based on the intention you stated at the outset of your week. In Full Focus Planner terms, it's the Weekly Big 3 tasks. For each, you ask three questions:

- How far did I get?
- What worked and what didn't?
- What will I keep, improve, start, or stop doing?

Being candid about this actually reduces anxiety about anything that didn't go well. It's not intended to fill you with guilt or feelings of failure. Instead, identifying solutions puts you back in control.

Sweep Your Lists. Here is where you review open items identified during your Friday Shutdown Ritual, plus delegated tasks, daily notes, and goals. Make note of any items that will need attention in the coming week. Add the rest to your master task list so you know they won't be missed later.

Create a Weekly Overview. Begin by listing to-do items that need attention, appointments, and deadlines. Then sketch your weekly schedule, deciding what to do on which days. This gives you a chance to prioritize, since you usually can't do everything you'd like to. You can decide well in advance which appointments you can commit to and which you'll reschedule.

Choose Your Weekly Big 3. Choose only three objectives that will advance your most important goals and projects during any one week. By doing this, you define your potential big wins for the week. If those three things get done, the week is a win, no matter what else happens.

Plan Your Self-Care. Finally, state your intention for self-care in five areas: sleep, eat, move, connect, and relax. This ensures that you don't pile on so many tasks that your health, relationships, and interests get squeezed out.

If you've not done this ritual before, allow yourself a full hour to complete it. With a little practice, you can get it down to between 20 and 30 minutes. That brief ritual will help you relax on the weekend and launch you into Monday with a solid plan for what you'll achieve, and when.

We highly recommend using this template for your own Weekly Preview. Regardless of how you structure yours, it's important to have a ritual for previewing your week. Enter the week without a plan and events will take control. Automate your weekly planning with this simple ritual and you'll never dread Monday again.

Get Ready for Peak Performance

At Michael Hyatt & Co., we believe you can win at work *and* succeed in life. We call that the Double Win. Michael created the BusinessAccelerator program to teach these principles to successful but overwhelmed business leaders. Four times each year, several groups of leaders gather to receive live coaching. The energy generated by a roomful of leaders intent on growing their businesses is amazing. Each cohort is a manageable size, so members get lots of peer interaction and personal attention. To achieve the intimate nature of live coaching, we generally run several days of back-to-back coaching intensives with a different cohort each day.

One recent stretch was particularly busy. Michael led coaching groups nine out of eleven days, delivering content and interacting with clients all morning, then again all afternoon. When he shared the schedule with friends, one was dumbfounded. "How on earth do you keep that schedule?" he asked. "I would *never* have the energy for that."

Michael told him the secret. "Every day, even during busy coaching sessions, I stick to my Midday Ritual." On coaching days, that means eating a nutritious lunch with the team, then retreating to the greenroom for a nap. "It gives me the recharge I need to keep teaching all day long."

We said it at the beginning and it's important to reiterate again—your time is fixed, but your energy flexes. Imagine how much more productive you might be if you could run at peak efficiency all day, week in and week out. Install these rejuvenation rituals and adapt them to fit your biorhythms. You'll get more done in less time and feel better doing it.

MOMENTUM BUILDER

Design Your Midday Ritual

The process for creating a Rejuvenation Ritual is essentially the same as for Daily Rituals. However, in this case, you may have little or no existing practices to build from. That's okay. Just follow the steps in this tool and you can design a ritual to meet any need. Begin with the most basic Rejuvenation Ritual, the Midday Ritual.

First, state your desired outcome. What would you like to be true after refreshing yourself midday? How do you want to feel? Describe your ideal state of mind and body when returning to work.

Second, catalog what you already do. If you don't have a fixed ritual, no problem. List the typical things you might do midday, such as go out for lunch, work at your desk, catch up on messages, or have a lunch meeting.

Third, identify what works and what doesn't. Critically examine each element of your ritual. Is it refreshing you? Is it depleting your energy? Could it be strengthened? Is anything missing from your list?

Fourth, reengineer as needed. Remove any items from your list that aren't working. Tweak those that could be more effective. And add any missing items that you need to help you reach your target. Then revise the order as needed, including the time needed.

Congratulations! You now have a solid ritual for midday rejuvenation. And you have a template for creating rituals for weekends, mealtimes, or any time you want to reboot your energy.

SELF-AUTOMATION

LEVEL 3

Design Templates to Automate Entire Days

7

Design the Day

To automate your day, you must understand the basic contexts in which you live and work, and arrange them to match your energy.

Suppose you bought a home for your young family. Let's say it was a lovely Victorian house in a quaint small town. The house was old, but very spacious and in great shape. With a few updates, it became the perfect place to raise a family. You planned to stay for many years.

Then, one by one, your kids grew up and moved out. Before long, grandchildren began to arrive. Within a few years, you realize that lovely old home is no longer adequate for your needs. You've got plenty of bedrooms, but no gathering space for your large, extended family. What would you do?

One option would be to move out of town and build a home. If you could find the right property and hire a custom builder, you could have exactly the home you need. After a bit of searching, you find a lovely site. You're excited about the possibility and ready to contact a builder. It's exciting.

Then you get that promotion you've long been seeking. The new job is wonderful, but it will require intense travel, especially at the beginning. After speaking with a builder, you realize the vast number of decisions required to create a custom home. Choosing a site is just the beginning. Then comes the floorplan, and the siding, and the roofing, and the mechanicals, and the flooring, and the finish, and the woodwork, and the paint, and the hardware, and the appliances, and the landscaping. All of these decisions on top of starting a new job is simply overwhelming. Reluctantly, you decide that building a custom home is simply out of the question. You're back to square one.

Your attention is forced back to your existing home, the one you fell in love with fifteen years ago. After consulting with an architect, you realize that by enclosing a porch and extending the kitchen just a couple of feet, you can create a great room where the whole family can gather. And adding a patio and grill to the backyard gives you a second gathering space for summer. The solution turns out to be remarkably simple and much less disruptive than you'd thought. With a few minor adjustments to the floorplan of your home, it is once again a perfect fit for your family.

What does this story have to do with automating your day? Actually, quite a bit.

Remodel Your Day

We're used to thinking of every day as a clean slate. It's a fresh start filled with possibilities. And that feels great. But it's also a problem. Every day brings a truckload of opportunities, problems, interruptions, distractions, projects, and messages. When we enter a day without a plan, it's like building a house from the ground up. It requires nonstop decisions about what to prioritize, who to spend time with, what you really want to accomplish, what you can't afford to include, and what to do next. It's exhausting and counterproductive.

The answer for designing your day is to think like a remodeler, not a builder. Begin with an existing plan rather than starting from scratch. When you have a solid template for each day, it's easy to make minor adjustments. You can tweak your plan just a bit to account for problems and opportunities that unexpectedly arise. And for the most part, each day moves effortlessly from one planned activity to the next.

Templates do for your entire day what Daily Rituals do for your morning and evening: automate them. Unlike your Daily Rituals, which remain relatively stable from day to day, you can choose a different template for each day, depending on what you want to accomplish. Do this and your day will go from interrupted, reactive, and stressed to calm and in control. You'll never again end the day asking, "What just happened?" And you'll be more productive than ever before. The first step to automating your day is to understand two fundamental things: the *contexts* in which you live and work and your mental *energy*.

Contexts

Nearly every home has three basic types of spaces: a kitchen, a bedroom, and a living room. There are others, of course, but those are the basics. And each one has its own purpose. You don't generally prepare food in the living room or sleep in the kitchen. In the same way, your days all contain three basic contexts. They're like rooms in a house. To create a template for your day, you need to be familiar with them and know what they're for. They will form the walls that keep your work life from overflowing into your personal life. They're also a barrier against the interruptions and distractions that destroy your focus.

Two of these contexts were first identified by Michael Gerber in The *E-Myth Revisited* and have been widely adopted in the business world. I added the third to highlight another important distinction in our daily lives.

In the Business

In the business is where you do the more routine parts of your work. Think of it like the kitchen of a house. Most of what you do in a kitchen is preparation for eating. And most of what you do when working "in" the business is preparation for the meatier parts of your job, the things that really drive results.

Working in the business involves things like attending meetings, responding to email, or proofreading a report. All are normal business activities. However, much of that activity doesn't directly advance the mission of your company. Sure, everyone needs to check messages and file expense reports, but that's probably not the work you were hired to do. It's background work.

Working *in* the business is not your primary work, but it supports the work that you were hired to do.

Often, we spend a little too much time in this context because it's actually easier than doing our real job. For example, tidying your workspace is important for keeping you productive. That's a perfectly acceptable use of your time. But when you spend an hour arranging paper clips, you've drifted into *downhill work*. As the name implies, this is work that is easier and less taxing than the deep work that drives results. Over-formatting spreadsheets, composing lengthy emails, and endlessly scrolling through your news feed are all downhill work.

Reserve as much of your day as needed but as little as possible for working in the business. Eliminate downhill work altogether.

On the Business

On the business is where you should spend most of your time. When you are working "on" the business, you're doing the things that actually move the company forward. If you are a business owner or leader, that's strategic planning, developing new products, communicating vision, and opening new markets.

Obviously, these are complex activities that entail a number of specific tasks. But unlike in the business tasks, these all involve directly fulfilling the company's mission.

Many employees are more narrowly focused on more specific work like sales, marketing, or operations. If that's you, you drive results by making sales calls, creating marketing campaigns, or responding to customer inquiries. Whenever you are doing the work you were hired to do, you're working *on* the business. That work deserves your best time and energy.

Out of the Business

When you are *out of the business*, you're not really working. We could label this "personal time." But clarifying this context as "out" of the business—think out of bounds—makes the context seem more like a boundary. When you work through lunch, check email after supper, or drag the laptop on vacation, you're crossing that boundary. It's like cooking pancakes in the bedroom. When you're working *in* the business or *on* it, the business deserves your full attention. When you're not, your attention belongs elsewhere.

We may justify crossing boundaries, saying, "But this is a critical project," or "If I don't do it, it won't get done." The most common excuse is "You don't understand, I love my job!" When you jump back into work rather than resting, exercising, or spending time with family and friends, it robs you of the rejuvenation you need to work at peak energy.

Given the fact that more and more of us are working remotely, it is even more vital to make this distinction. Automating your day requires setting clear boundaries within your work—working on versus working in the business—and around your work hours. Do this so you can be out of business even if your work is in the same place as your personal time.

Using these three basic contexts, you can create any number of templates. Some days may be spent working either in, on, or out of the business. Others will be a mix. You might have one template for a "Meeting Day," another for a "Deep Work Day," and one for a "Day Off." The important thing is to clarify the boundary between these specific types of days. And to do that, we need to explain another vital consideration in designing your day: your energy.

Energy

Have you ever noticed that some rooms in your home are more pleasant at different times of day?

An east-facing kitchen may feel perky in the morning but a bit dreary in late afternoon. And that beautiful deck with southern exposure is bound to get brutally hot on a summer afternoon. Every house has its own energy.

Chronotypes

People do, too. Everyone has a sleep cycle called a circadian rhythm, as we learned briefly in chapter 6. However, not everyone's rhythm is exactly the same. Behavioral scientists have identified several variations called *chronotypes*. You're probably familiar with two of these, popularly referred to as early birds and night owls. Clinical psychologist Michael J. Breus describes a total of four chronotypes. You'll probably see yourself somewhere in these brief descriptions.

Bear. The Bear chronotype follows the sun the most closely. People with this chronotype usually have no trouble falling asleep, and they feel the most energetic before noon. They have a predictable dip in energy after lunch, usually around two o'clock.

Wolf. People with this chronotype often sleep very late and enjoy their peak productivity in the afternoon. Their slump usually comes in the late afternoon. They may get a second wind around six o'clock and find themselves productive again in the evening.

Lion. People with this chronotype are early risers. Their energy is highest in the early morning and may be nonexistent later in the day. Lions may go to bed around nine or ten o'clock in the evening.

Dolphin. Those with this chronotype have trouble maintaining a regular pattern of sleep. Their peak energy is often around midday.

If you don't think any of these descriptions fit you, that's okay. The important thing is not to label yourself but to become aware of your own sleep-wake pattern and how that affects your energy throughout the day. When you understand your own rhythm, you can plan your work accordingly.

If you have a traditional workweek of five eight-hour days, you may not have absolute freedom to structure your time every day. The secret is to work "on" the business during your peak energy hours as much as you can. Freelancers, gig workers, and those who work from home or in a hybrid context may have more freedom.

The traditional workday was not handed down from the mountain. It was invented during the Industrial Age to get the greatest productivity from each worker during a 24-hour day. But knowledge workers simply cannot operate consistently at peak energy for eight hours. If you can, automate your days, structuring your activity in, on, and out of the business to take advantage of your natural rhythms.

Draw the Lines

Michael and his wife, Gail, love their new home. It's the same Victorian house they fell in love with decades ago, but the few adjustments have made it seem more vibrant and useful than ever. It saved them the hard work of designing a house, seeing it through construction, and moving. During the years that followed, by deciding to stay in their home instead starting from scratch, Michael Hyatt & Co. grew by 162 percent, in part because Michael was able to give it his full attention.

What would your life look like if you could apply those same principles to your work? How much more would you enjoy each day if it were not fragmented to bits, with work constantly invading your personal space and vice versa? Imagine how productive you could be if you were freed to focus on your "real job" when you felt most energetic and creative.

That's the way your days *will* be when you create templates around the contexts of your work and life and align them with your natural energy. Separating those spaces is the first step to automating your day. The next step is to populate them with tasks.

MOMENTUM BUILDER

Map Your Week

The first step to creating a template (or several templates) for your day is to map a typical week. Begin with a weekly calendar, either electronic or analog, including all seven days.

First, plot your typical sleep pattern. Shade those hours gray.

Second, add the hours when you are most alert and energetic. Shade those hours green. You can lighten or darken the shading to indicate intensity if you like. This will be an estimate based on your typical pattern.

Third, add the hours when you are less focused and energetic. Shade those times yellow. Again, you can vary the shading (or use a different color) to indicate the times when your energy is at its absolute lowest.

Do you see patterns emerging? You may notice your high energy periods as a green band running horizontally across every morning, afternoon, or evening. Or you might see a vertical pattern, with high and low energy alternating throughout the day. Either is fine. Just become aware of when you focus the best so you can plan your days accordingly.

Fourth, draw the boundaries for each of the three contexts in which you are active. If you're using a paper calendar, actually draw lines around each block of time. On an electronic calendar, you can create appointments with yourself for those blocks of time.

- Begin with out of the business time. It's important to draw those lines first, so you protect your margin and avoid overwork. Include your Daily Rituals and Rejuvenation Rituals. Those times must be protected also.
- Next, set your targets for working on the business. Sync this with your high energy periods as much as you can, though you may have to include some lower-energy periods also. Don't worry about conflicts with your existing schedule. We'll cover those in the next chapter.
- Finally, schedule your in the business time. Do your best to sync them with your energy peaks and valleys.

This weekly map will become the basis for the daily templates you create.

8

Batch the Tasks

To complete your daily template, arrange tasks for maximum efficiency using four types of batching.

Online orders have become commonplace in the past few years—but something about waiting for a delivery still seems to bring out the inner kid in people. We can't wait for the just released book or newest piece of gear to turn up on our doorsteps. And now that UPS offers real-time tracking of deliveries, you can see the truck's position on a map and countdown the minutes until arrival.

But have you ever noticed that sometimes the UPS driver passes your house once, even twice without stopping—with your package on board—only to show up an hour later with your delivery? It seems terribly inefficient. Why not stop at the first opportunity?

According to a former industrial engineer at UPS, there's a good reason for that. Each driver's daily stops are carefully planned by type, such as residential or business, and those requiring a signature release. Each stop is allotted a certain amount of time based on the type of stop and the number of packages. This accounts for everything down to the smallest of details: the time needed to drive to the address, turn off the ignition, undo the seat belt, open the bulkhead door, retrieve the package, exit the vehicle, walk to the door, leave the package, walk back to the vehicle, put on the seat belt, and start the engine. A residential stop might be allowed thirty seconds, often much less. And the driver might make up to 190 stops a day and deliver 200 or more packages.

Each day's route is pre-planned to take advantage of natural traffic patterns and avoid complicated turns. Then the truck is loaded in a way that makes it easier for the driver to retrieve the right packages in the right order. So, when the driver hops into the truck and turns the key, he is completely free to focus on two things: safe driving and efficient delivery. As you follow the truck's progress online, it looks random and haphazard. But, in fact, the entire process has been carefully planned to maximize the driver's time and energy. A single driver is now equipped to make all those stops and deliver all those packages.

A truly haphazard approach would be to toss packages into the truck as quickly as possible, then leave the driver to spend the day making decision after decision about where to go next. Yet, that's exactly what most of us do every day. We arrive at work brimming with energy and dive into the most urgent or obvious task, then scramble to keep up all day long. Like UPS figured out, there is a better way to do our knowledge work.

The Power of Batching

By now, you understand the three contexts in which all your activities take place: in, on, or out of your business. And you understand something about the rhythm of your day. You know when your energy and focus are at their best. What remains is to structure the day itself, so that the right tasks get done at the right time. To finish your template, you'll need to think like a delivery driver planning the most efficient route. Maximizing efficiencies requires mastering the technique of *batching*. Your day will flow seamlessly from one activity to the next when you leverage four types of batching.

Simple Batching

Batching is a very simple idea. It means grouping like activities together. That way, you make more efficient use of your time and get more done. But there's a bit more to it than simply doing all your in the business work at one time and your on the business work at another. That's because the tasks within those contexts may be very different.

Research by Sophie Leroy of the University of Washington shows that our brains find it difficult to switch between tasks. While we may begin the new task, part of our mind remains fixed on the prior one. That "attention residue" degrades our performance on both tasks. That's why you're more likely to make mistakes while texting during a meeting or replying to an urgent email when interrupted from entering data. Your body can't be in two places at once and, as it turns out, your brain can't either.

Batching, in its simplest form, means grouping like tasks together. It reduces the cost of task switching, saving you time and energy. Fielding Slack questions from team members, responding to email, and filing reports are in the business tasks. But while two of them involve communication, the other is clerical. To batch them, you might set aside a half hour to empty your inboxes, then turn off chat and email notifications, and spend the next half hour generating your expense report and weekly sales report. Structuring your tasks this way keeps your mental energy in the same space for longer amounts of time. And it keeps you using the same apps or programs for several tasks in a row. This method reduces the cost of task switching.

To batch your tasks, try grouping them by these factors:

- Context—in, on, or out of the business
- Type—clerical, communication, deep thought, meetings, etc.
- Energy Use—high or low
- Time—shorter or longer

The less you switch tasks, or switch from one headspace to another, the better your day will flow.

Horizontal Batching

When you plotted your energy on a weekly calendar

in chapter 7, you may have noticed a clear pattern of green, yellow, and gray running horizontally across the page. That indicates that you have a fairly consistent pattern of energy each day of the week. For a Lion chronotype, that would probably look like a big green stripe across the morning hours, fading to yellow by afternoon, and switching to gray in mid-evening. For a Wolf, the gray area might extend into mid-morning with a bright green stripe across every early afternoon and late evening. Whatever the case, you may see that you have periods of high or low energy at about the same times each day. Horizontal batching takes advantage of those peaks and valleys by scheduling the same kinds of activities every day around the same time.

If you have higher energy in the morning, you'll probably schedule on the business work before lunch and in the business work in the afternoon. That might mean, for example, scheduling meetings only in the afternoon. Or, you might work from home most mornings to minimize interruptions. If your energy peaks later in the day, you might spend the morning on communication, administrative work, and other tasks that require less energy. Then, you can dive into writing, strategic planning, or sales calls in the afternoon when you're rearing to go.

By default, your Daily Rituals are batched horizontally. A ritual is already a batch of tasks. In this case, they are our habits. And their value is in adding structure to each day. With the possible exception of your out of the business days, rituals will be performed at roughly the same time each day.

Freelancers, contractors, or anyone who determines their own schedule will have the most latitude in batching horizontally. The point is to avoid using your precious mental focus on tasks that don't drive results in your work.

Vertical Batching

When you plotted your energy on a weekly calendar, you may have noticed a vertical rather than horizontal pattern. It's possible that you find it easier to concentrate on certain days of the week rather than the same time every day. For example, many people find Mondays or Fridays to be low-energy days. Or your energy pattern may not be pronounced enough to make horizontal batching worthwhile. If either scenario describes you, vertical batching is another way to structure your time to maximize your focus.

Vertical batching is grouping tasks by day of the week rather than time of day. Our leaders at Michael

Hyatt & Co. do this with meetings. Some meetings qualify as working in the business. That includes things like staff meetings and one-on-one meetings with direct reports. Others are working on the business, like meetings with potential clients or partners, strategic planning meetings, or vision casting with the team.

We batch meetings vertically whenever possible. On Mondays and Fridays, we use a Meeting Day template. Mondays are generally reserved for in the business meetings. For our executives, those may begin at nine o'clock in the morning and run back-to-back all day with breaks, of course. Those meetings requiring the most energy are usually scheduled in the morning.

External meetings are batched on Fridays. This grouping of meetings typically concerns on the business work, such as meetings with prospective clients or partners, or scheduled calls or video conferences aimed at expanding the reach of our business.

Most people find it easier to switch from one meeting to another than from meeting to writing to meeting to focused thought. By batching vertically, you can keep yourself in the same context for the entire day, which helps maintain focus. Vertical days run smoother and require much less energy than a day of constant task switching.

Megabatching

Megabatching puts the concept of batching into overdrive by reserving an entire day, or even multiple days, for a *single* task. We use megabatching for a number of tasks, notably podcast and video production here at Michael Hyatt & Co. One strategy for media production would be to batch recordings horizontally. That might mean recording for an hour each morning at ten o'clock, or every Tuesday from eleven to noon. That would make good use of morning energy. But it would disrupt the flow of several days in a typical month.

Instead, we batch all recordings for a particular project into one or two days. Whenever possible, we go from nine in the morning until five in the afternoon with a break for lunch. We will block as many days as it takes to complete the whole recording project. Megabatching requires careful energy management during those days. But it keeps us from doing a major task switch daily. It also frees the team from the interruptions they might encounter if carrying out other responsibilities that same day. Megabatching works well for writing, planning, sales calls, or anything requiring a significant period of focused attention.

Running the Route

Let's return to the example of the delivery driver. Like you, the driver operates in a specific area or context. But that alone doesn't ensure efficiency. It's planning the route that really moves the process along.

When you learn to batch your tasks, then leverage the power of horizontal, vertical, and megabatching, you'll pick up speed, too. There will be less friction in your day, less energy drain from task switching, and you'll find yourself more productive than ever before. How would you like to end each day thinking, "That was fun!" rather than, "I'll never do that again"? Use templates to automate your day, and you will end each day on a positive note.

Of course a plan is only as good as its execution. Your final step in self-automation is to master the steps to installing these templates into your day.

MOMENTUM BUILDER

Batch Your Tasks

Batch your tasks by following these simple steps. Don't overthink. This exercise is intended to get you started with batching. You can revise schedules as needed to arrive at a batching system that works for you.

First, list the things you do routinely. Don't evaluate, just write them down as you think of them.

Second, transfer the items to another list, this time batching them by the type of task or level of concentration required. You might use categories like these, or add your own.

- In the Business
- On the Business
- Meetings
- Communication
- Administrative
- Research
- Writing
- Planning
- Deep Work
- Consultation
- Oversight
- Collaboration

Third, number the groups of tasks according to the type of batching that would be most effective for them.

1. Simple Batching	Small tasks that require the same kinds of focus
2. Horizontal Batching	Tasks that might be done at the same time each day
3. Vertical Batching	Tasks that might be done all on a single day
4. Megabatching	Tasks that might be done on a single day or consecutive days

Finally, return to the weekly map you created in chapter 7. Pencil in your batched tasks. For example, you might write "Communication" on each weekday at two o'clock. Or you designate every Friday for "Strategic Planning." Think of this as an experiment. Try it for a week, then make adjustments as needed.

9

Install the Template

To ensure that your template does not conflict with coworkers or family members, use a four-step activation plan

When Michael Hyatt & Co. began, there was only one employee: Michael. Within a short time, he saw the need for a part-time executive assistant, then another. As the business continued to grow, so did the team. Today, we have thirty-eight full-time employees. And as we grew, the complexity of our work expanded, too. We soon found ourselves struggling to protect the time needed for deep work, as the time spent on meetings and other in the business tasks continued to grow. We understood that deep, focused work was driving the growth of our company, and we couldn't afford to lose it.

Our solution was to adopt a very basic weekly rhythm for the entire company. Essentially, this meant coordinating our various templates around a couple of key days when we would all use the same one. Our leadership team moved all internal meetings to Mondays. And they decided to vertically batch some of our on the business tasks on a single day. That became known as Meeting-Free Thursday, though we later changed it to Wednesday. With surprisingly few exceptions, we have no meetings company-wide on Wednesdays. That means no one-on-ones, no team training, no sprints, no meetings of any kind.

The effect on our productivity was dramatic. No Meeting Wednesday has become a shared experience we look forward to each week. Slack messages slow to a trickle. So does the traffic in our coworking space. Having no meetings to attend, many team members choose to work from home the entire day. Others take advantage of the slower pace to engage in deep, focused work in the office. Most important, since implementing these changes, productivity has increased sharply. Together, the entire team automated our week—and our company is better for it.

Activate Your Template

Few people work in isolation. Most of us must coordinate our schedule with coworkers, family members, partners, and even clients and customers. If your templates are to be something other than a good idea, it must be activated in your real-life context. Like a habit or daily ritual, templates must be brought to life by action. As with habits and rituals, there's a simple process for it, we call it a template loop. Complete the automation of your day by activating your template in four simple steps. When you do, you'll avoid conflict, minimize interruptions, and see a huge increase in your ability to focus.

Calendar Your Template

What gets scheduled gets done. This is a statement Michael has made countless times. Yet, we're certain some will be reading those words for the first time. The easiest way to install a template into your life is to put it on your schedule. We mean literally writing the contexts of your day on the calendar, like an appointment, then populate them with tasks, inducing your Daily Rituals. Your calendar becomes the activation trigger that puts your automated day in motion.

Generally, things take a bit longer than we think they will. So, when we have only a vague idea that we will "focus on deep work in the morning," we usually overestimate what we can accomplish. Some tasks get pushed to the afternoon, or to the next day, and we're right back where we started: reactive, stressed, and out of control.

Start by writing "Morning Ritual" in the time slot you intend to do it. Do the same with your Startup and Shutdown Rituals. Then, slot your non-discretionary time. That's the time you've already committed (or had committed for you) to meetings, travel, and whatever else you have pre-planned for the week. Finally, schedule the first batch of tasks you want to accomplish, and then the next batch after that. When executed well, you're essentially batching your decision making about the order in which to tackle your tasks. That accomplishes two things. First, it helps you correctly estimate how long a task really takes. Second, it keeps you from wondering "What should I do next?" every half hour. Your day will flow as it's supposed to.

This template won't be the same for every day, of course. You'll have a range of templates to choose from, like Meeting Day, Deep Work Day, Travel Day, and so on. Choose your template for the next day during your Workday Shutdown Ritual and map it on your calendar.

If this practice feels uncomfortable to you, think of it like training wheels. In time, your templates will be so firmly installed that you won't need to consciously think about which template will be best for which day. It will run automatically.

Plan for Interruptions

Did you know that on most days, you can actually plan your interruptions? Yes, really. That's because most of them are highly predictable. For example, your mind and body will tell you it's time for a break every sixty to ninety minutes. Since you know that, you can add those breaks to your template. Don't schedule back-to-back meetings without at least a ten-minute break. Or, adopt the fifty-minute hour to build breaks into your day.

Most interruptions from team members are also predictable. Allow time in the day for returning messages. Put it into the template so you won't be tempted to check email due to a sense of urgency.

Your Workday Startup and Shutdown Rituals are a good place to start.

Coordinate with Others

As we discovered at Michael Hyatt & Co., it's difficult to implement your own template when it conflicts with others.' Yet, most people are willing to flex a bit so everyone has time to work on the business. Here are some ways of coordinating your templates with family members and coworkers.

Adopt Common Terms. It helps when everyone understands what you mean by being in, on, or out of the business. Whatever you choose to call your high-leverage work, communicate that with the people around you. For example, when you say, "I need some time for deep work," they'll understand that you mean intense focus and be more likely to give you some space.

Negotiate Commitments. By commitments, we mean primarily meetings and deliverables. There may be some meetings you don't need to attend if you'll agree to read the minutes, or others you can opt out of entirely. At a minimum, you may be able to reschedule some meetings away from your peak performance hours. The same with deliverables. When possible, negotiate deadlines that allow you to batch your work and maintain focus.

Signal Availability. Find ways to signal to let others know when you're available and when you're not. In our company, we use the status signal on Slack to communicate when we're in a meeting, at lunch, doing deep work, traveling, or on PTO. And one area of our coworking space is designated for deep work. Working in that room rather than at a common table indicates that you don't want to be disturbed.

If you work in a traditional office, you might use earbuds to signal that your attention is occupied, or even post a good-natured sign on your cubicle. If your office doesn't have a culture of signaling unavailability, start one.

This is especially important for those of us working from home. Family members may be less likely to understand that you don't want to be disturbed, especially children. Let them know the specific times you'll be available and when you need uninterrupted focus. Predictability is key. When others have confidence that they'll have access to you at consistent times, they're more likely to honor your schedule.

Iterate

As with habits and rituals, templates will work

automatically once you get them installed. Also, like habits and rituals, they may not perform perfectly on the first try. It takes up to eight weeks to install a habit. And Daily Rituals are always a work in progress. You need to initiate your templates, then keep adjusting until they run automatically.

Your first step is to try it. Calendar your template, communicate it to others, and give it a go. A template does no good inside your head. It must be implemented in real-time.

Then, optimize your template. The very first day you try using a template, you'll probably find ways to improve it. Don't be discouraged! That's perfectly normal. In fact, it would be surprising if you didn't hit a few snags. If horizontal batching doesn't work for you, try vertical batching. If you find yourself getting fatigued, reexamine your break schedule. These templates reflect *your* ideal days. You can change them any way you like. Make some adjustments and run it again. Keep optimizing each template until it works for you consistently.

Finally, keep at it. Some days get disrupted, and that's okay. You may have a meeting scheduled on short notice, a task may take much longer than expected, or a problem may arise with a customer. These things happen. Your template will be interrupted from time to time. If you complete your ideal day about 80 percent of the time, you're doing great. When things don't go as planned one day, get a good night's sleep and start fresh the next day.

Set It in Motion

Your life is already running on autopilot. You already have habits. You already have daily rituals. And, likely, you already have templates. If you've read this far, it's likely that those habits, rituals, and templates aren't producing the results you want.

So, the question is not "Can I practice self-automation?" Yes, you can. Everyone does already. The real question is whether you'll get the results you're looking for. Can you develop the habits that lead to a healthier and more productive life? Yes, you can. Can you install Daily Rituals that will run automatically, giving your days a foundation for success? Of course. Can you design your days so that they unfold as if by magic, with one activity flowing seamlessly to the next while you become more focused and productive than ever? Absolutely. You can do this.

We've seen it hundreds of times before in our coaching clients. When business leaders enter our BusinessAccelerator program, many of them feel just like you. They're overcapacity, overwhelmed, reactive, and fighting for control of their business's health and personal wellbeing. These very same principles shared in this book are among the things we teach them. And when these leaders put them into practice, the results are immediate and dramatic. We've heard tearfully joyful testimonials from clients who reduced their work from more than sixty hours a week to less than forty. Others have reconnected with spouses and children, dramatically increased their income, and rediscovered passion for their work.

You can experience that same transformation. It begins when you take control of your habits, rituals, and daily routines. You have everything you need to start this journey. And we believe you will.

You've got this.

MOMENTUM BUILDER

Activation Success Worksheet

One of the best ways to ensure that you actually take an action is to make a written plan. Your final challenge is to state your intention to implement self-automation at each of the three levels: habits, rituals, and templates.

Be intentional here, but don't drift into the delusion zone. You can absorb a limited amount of change at one time. Even so, having a written plan will make you much more likely to succeed in automating your days. We recommend installing only one habit, set of rituals, and daily template during a single quarter.

Level 1: Habits

- What habit will you activate first? List the activation trigger, response, reward, and repetition (frequency and duration).
- When will you begin?
- How will you track this habit?
- When will you evaluate your progress?
- What will you do to celebrate your success? When will you do it?
- Add the start, end, review, and celebration dates to your calendar.

Level 2: Rituals

- Begin with the four Daily Rituals. List the steps of each of them, in order, with a time estimate for each step.
- State the activation trigger for each of the four rituals.
- What schedule alterations do you need to make in order to activate these rituals?
- When will you make those changes?

- Who else must you coordinate with or keep informed, and when will you communicate with them?
- On what date will you conduct a review of your rituals to optimize them?
- How long will you track the rituals before you consider them installed?
- What will you do to celebrate your success? When will you do it?
- Add the start, end, review, and celebration dates to your calendar.

* *Repeat this process for your Rejuvenation Rituals, or any other rituals you'd like to create.*

Level 3: Templates

- Determine what type of templates you need to automate your typical week.
- Which template will you implement first?
- What schedule alterations do you need to make in order to activate this template?
- When will you make those changes?
- Who else must you coordinate with or keep informed and when will you communicate with them?
- What interruptions do you anticipate?
- How and when will you schedule these interruptions?

- How will you signal your availability or unavailability?
- When will you activate this template?
- On what date will you conduct a review to optimize this template?
- How long will you track the effectiveness of this template before you consider it fully installed?
- What will you do to celebrate your success? When will you do it?
- Add the template to your calendar.

* *Repeat this process for your Rejuvenation Rituals, or any other rituals you'd like to create.*

Sources

Roy F. Baumeister & Kathleen D. Vohs, "Misguided Effort with Elusive Implications," *Psychological Science*, March 2016, https://www.psychologicalscience.org/redesign/wp-content/uploads/2016/03/RRR-comment-BaumeisterVohs-revised-March17-002.pdf.

Leah Bitsky, "Richard Branson Reveals His Go-To Outfit for Any Occasion," *Page Six*, May 29, 2019, https://pagesix.com/2019/05/29/richard-branson-reveals-his-go-to-outfit-for-any-occasion.

Mason Currey, *Daily Rituals: How Artists Work* (New York: Knopf, 2013), xiv.

Daniel Engber, "Everything Is Crumbling," *Slate*, March 6, 2016, http://www.slate.com/articles/

health_and_science/cover_story/2016/03/ego_depletion_an_influential_theory_in_psychology_may_have_just_been_debunked.html?wpsrc=sh_all_dt_tw_top.

Marqui Mapp, "Dressing for Success, Using the Exact Same Outfit," *CNBC*, July 6, 2016, https://www.cnbc.com/2015/05/16/dress-for-success-by-wearing-same-thing-daily-melinda-kahl.html.

Joe Pinsker, "Why People Get the 'Sunday Scaries,'" *The Atlantic*, February 9, 2020, https://www.theatlantic.com/family/archive/2020/02/sunday-scaries-anxiety-workweek/606289/#:~:text=A%20 2018%20survey%20commissioned%20by,than%20 that%20for%20many%20people.

Maia Szalavitz, "Mind over Mind? Decision Fatigue Saps Willpower—if We Let It," *Time*, August 23, 2011, https://healthland.time.com/2011/08/23/mind-over-mind-decision-fatigue-may-deplete-our-willpower-but-only-if-we-let-it.

Mariel Tishma, "Conquering Attention Residue," *Chief Learning Officer*, March 2, 2018, https://

www.chieflearningofficer.com/2018/03/02/conquering-attention-residue.

Eric Torrence, "Why It Matters that Your Best Ideas Come in the Shower," *Thin Difference*, January 27, 2018, https://www.thindifference.com/2018/01/best-ideas-come-shower/.

Wendy Wood, *Good Habits, Bad Habits* (New York: Farrar, Straus, and Giroux, 2019), 27.

Mark Zuckerburg, "Q&A with Mark," *Facebook*, November 6, 2014, https://www.facebook.com/watch/?v=828790510512059.

About Michael Hyatt & Co.

Featured in the Inc. 5000 list as one of the fastest growing private companies in the nation three years in a row, Michael Hyatt & Co. is a leadership development firm helping successful, overwhelmed leaders get the focus they need to win at work and succeed at life.

Michael Hyatt & Co. has produced incredible products and satisfied hundreds of thousands of customers. They are the creators of the Full Focus Planner™ and the BusinessAccelerator® coaching program.

Our founder, Michael Hyatt, a *New York Times* bestselling author and entrepreneur, spent thirty-four years in the book publishing industry prior to establishing Michael Hyatt & Company in 2011. Over the course of his career, he worked in a variety of areas, including sales, editorial, marketing, and executive leadership, including serving as the CEO of the largest faith-based publisher in the world.

Learn more at **MichaelHyatt.com**.

PLAN YOUR YEAR, DESIGN YOUR DAYS, ACHIEVE YOUR BIGGEST GOALS

Escape the tyranny of the neverending to-do list. Use the Full Focus Planner to organize your priorities, make progress on what matters, and achieve your big goals. Learn more at **FullFocusPlanner.com**.

- Offers tactical solutions to act on your highest priorities, both day-to-day and year-to-year.
- Designed to keep your priorities in clear view, so that you set your course, stay on track, and achieve what matters every day.
- Crafted with sewn binding, ribbon markers, high-quality paper, and clutter-free design—the perfect combination of elegance and function.

Aesthetically pleasing, thoughtfully crafted, uniquely effective.